HUNTSMAN SPIDERS

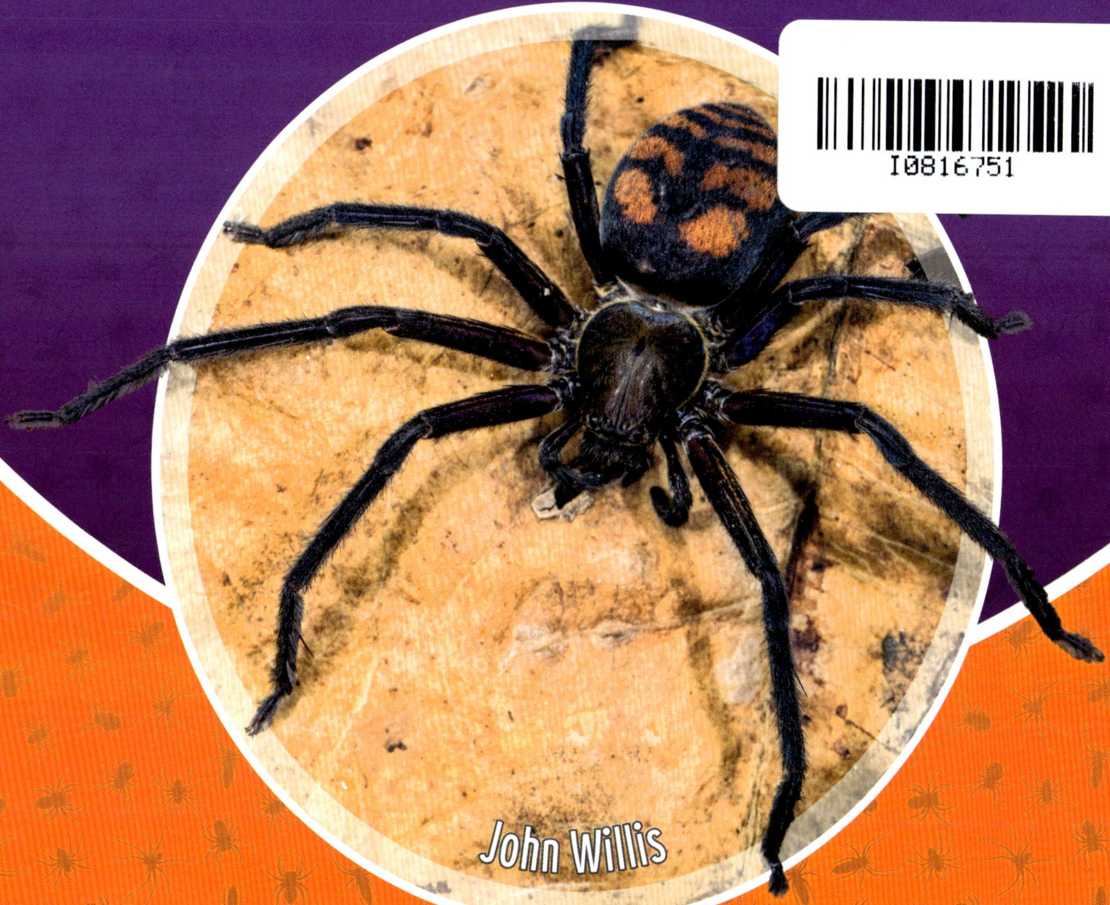

John Willis

SPIDERS

www.av2books.com

Step 1
Go to **www.av2books.com**

Step 2
Enter this unique code
FPVAI5UVH

Step 3
Explore your interactive eBook!

AV2 is optimized for use on any device

Your interactive eBook comes with...

Contents
Browse a live contents page to easily navigate through resources

Audio
Listen to sections of the book read aloud

Videos
Watch informative video clips

Weblinks
Gain additional information for research

Try This!
Complete activities and hands-on experiments

Key Words
Study vocabulary, and complete a matching word activity

Quizzes
Test your knowledge

Slideshows
View images and captions

... and much, much more!

SPIDERS

HUNTSMAN SPIDERS

Contents

Introduction

The Quick Huntsman Spider

Huntsman spiders get their name because they chase after their food. Like all spiders, they are animals with eight legs. Huntsman spiders are known for their large size and fast speed.

Most huntsman spiders are brown or gray. However, they can be found in many other colors.

Parts of a Spider
Spinnerets
Eyes
Fangs
Pedipalps
Legs

What Huntsman Spiders Look Like

Huntsman spiders have long, hairy legs and flat bodies. Each huntsman spider has eight eyes in two rows. Some huntsman spiders are small, but many are large. The biggest could cover a dinner plate with its legs. People often confuse large huntsman spiders with **tarantulas**.

There are more than
1,200 kinds
of huntsman spiders.
The average huntsman
spider's body is
0.7 inches
(1.8 centimeters) long.

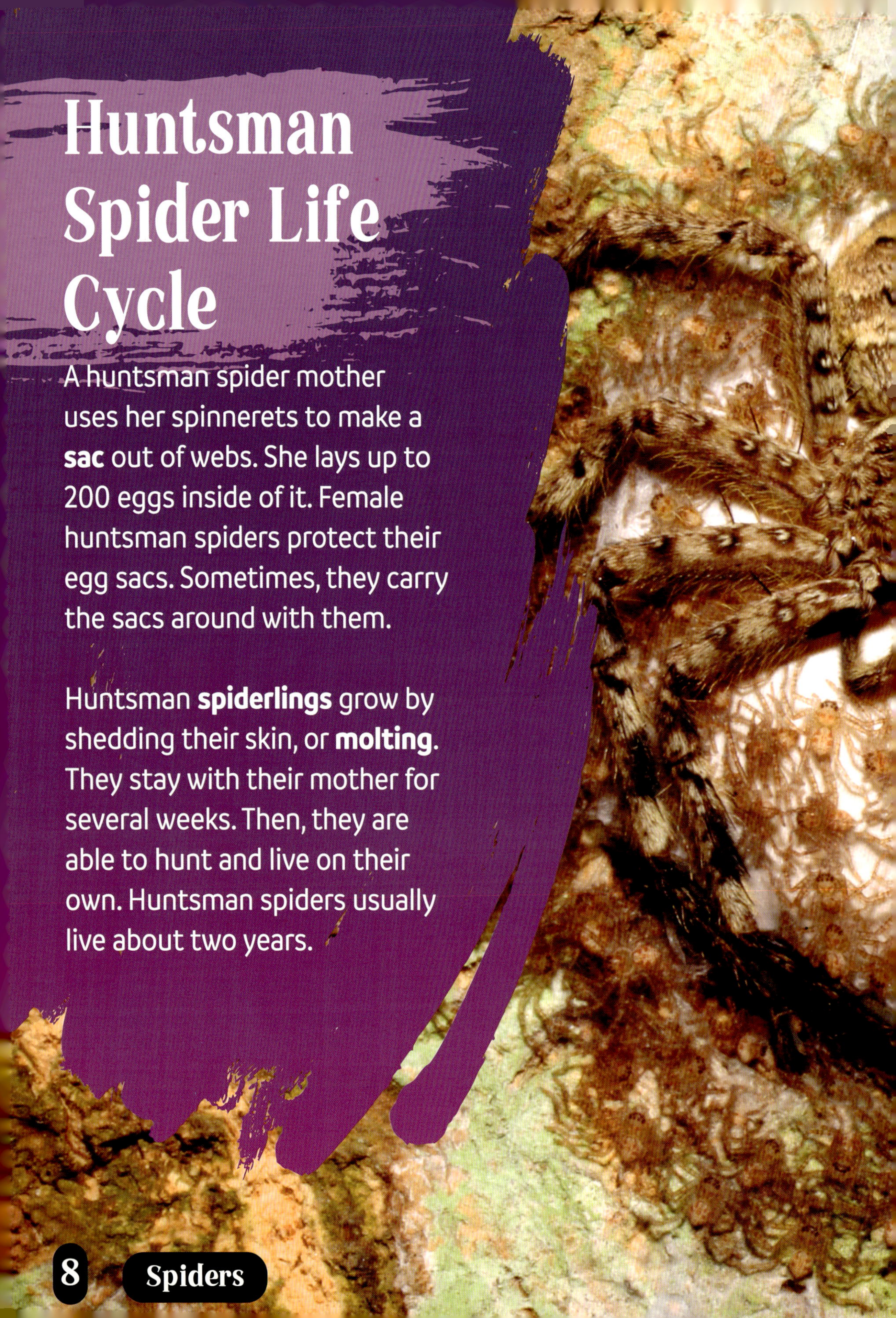

Huntsman Spider Life Cycle

A huntsman spider mother uses her spinnerets to make a **sac** out of webs. She lays up to 200 eggs inside of it. Female huntsman spiders protect their egg sacs. Sometimes, they carry the sacs around with them.

Huntsman **spiderlings** grow by shedding their skin, or **molting**. They stay with their mother for several weeks. Then, they are able to hunt and live on their own. Huntsman spiders usually live about two years.

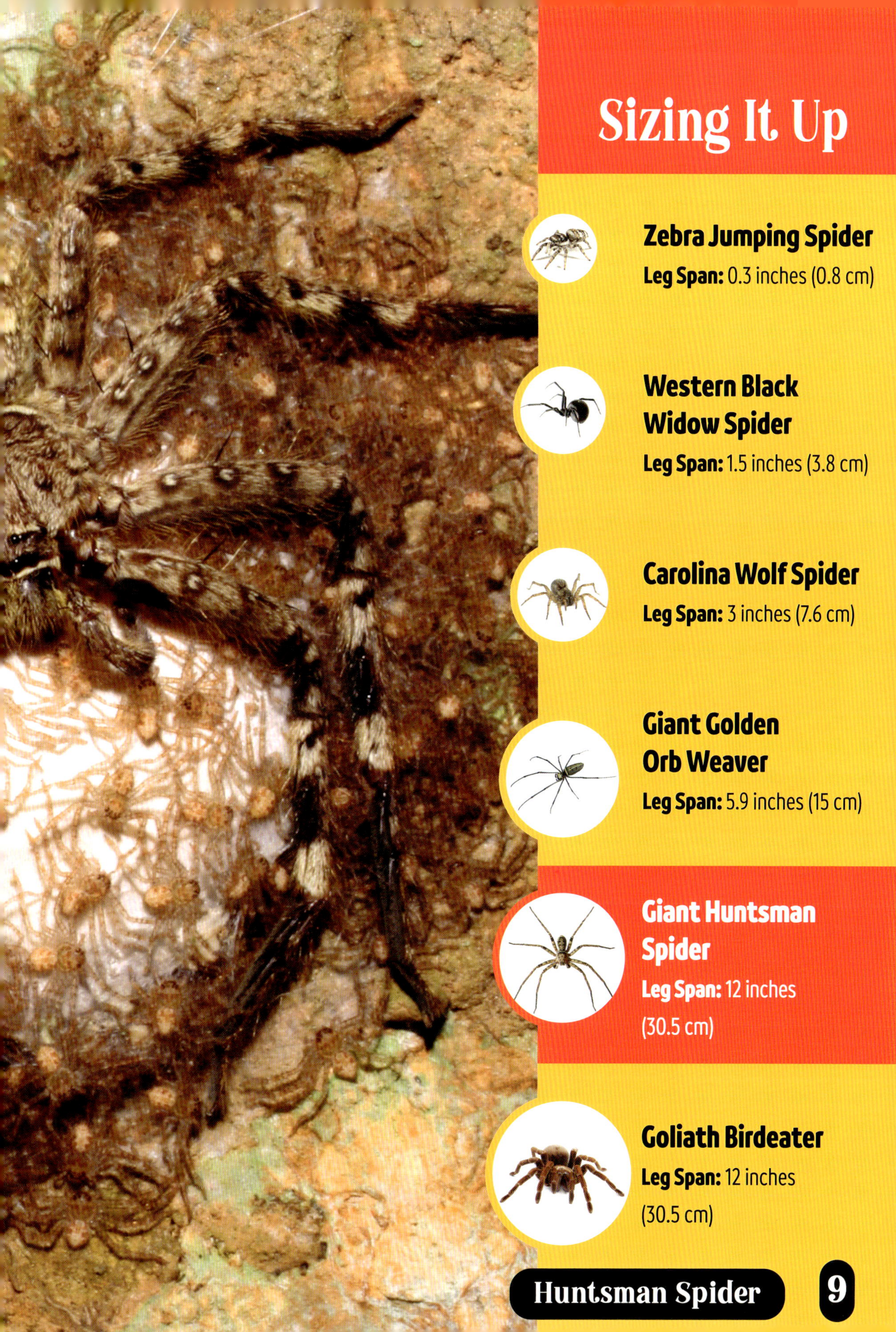

Sizing It Up

Zebra Jumping Spider
Leg Span: 0.3 inches (0.8 cm)

Western Black Widow Spider
Leg Span: 1.5 inches (3.8 cm)

Carolina Wolf Spider
Leg Span: 3 inches (7.6 cm)

Giant Golden Orb Weaver
Leg Span: 5.9 inches (15 cm)

Giant Huntsman Spider
Leg Span: 12 inches (30.5 cm)

Goliath Birdeater
Leg Span: 12 inches (30.5 cm)

Flat Spiders

A huntsman spider's body has a flat shape. This helps it get into tight spaces. Many huntsman spiders spend most of their lives underneath rocks or tree bark. Some huntsman spiders are colored to match their **habitat**. They hide on rocks, trees, or other plants.

Huntsman Spider

Twisted Legs

Huntsman spiders are often called "giant crab spiders" because of their legs. Huntsman spider legs are twisted where they connect to the body. This makes them spread out flat and to the side. The front legs are longer than the back ones. This lets huntsman spiders run forward and sideways quickly.

Huntsman Spider

Speedy Hunters

Huntsman spiders do not use webs to hunt. Instead, they chase after small animals. They grab their **prey** with their legs and **pedipalps**, then bite it with their **fangs**. To find food, huntsman spiders use their **senses**. They have better eyesight than most other spiders. The hairs on their legs help them sense **vibrations**.

In **2012**, people discovered **eyeless huntsman spiders**. They live in dark caves.

Huntsman spiders can **move 30 times their body length in one second.**

Map

Where They Live

Huntsman spiders are found all over the world. Many live in places that are warm all year. These include Australia and parts of the United States. Each huntsman spider has **adaptations** that help it live in its home.

Huntsman Spiders around the World

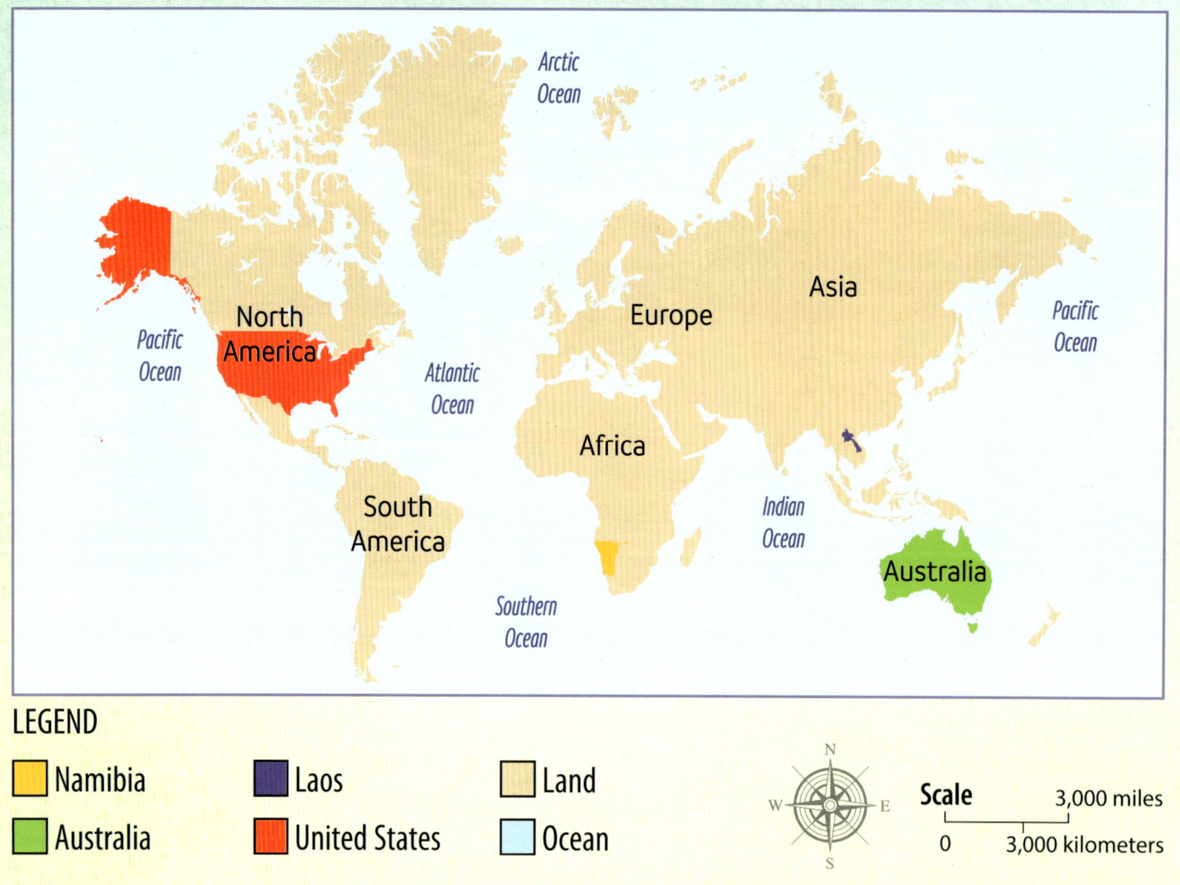

Giant Huntsman Spider

The giant huntsman spider was discovered in a cave in Laos in 2001. It is one of the largest spiders on Earth.

Pantropical Huntsman Spider

Pantropical huntsman spiders may have arrived in the United States inside crates of bananas. Today, they are often known as "banana spiders."

Social Huntsman Spider

Most huntsman spiders live alone. However, Australia's social huntsman spiders live in groups of up to 300.

Wheel Spider

Wheel spiders live in deserts in African countries such as Namibia. These huntsman spiders escape from danger by curling up and rolling down steep **sand dunes**.

Huntsman Spider Safety

Huntsman spiders are helpful animals. They eat **pests** such as cockroaches. Huntsman spiders are not dangerous. They usually try to run away from people. However, their bites can be very painful. To safely move a huntsman spider, put a container over it. Then, slide something flat, such as paper, under the container. Next, let the spider go outside.

Activity

Create a Spider

There are many different kinds of spiders in the world. They all have certain features in common. However, each spider also has its own features. They help the spider live in its home.

Make your own spider by answering the following questions:

1. What is your spider called?
2. Where does it live?
3. What features does it share with other spiders?
4. What features help it live in its home? How do these features do this?
5. What does your spider look like?
6. Use pencils, markers, or crayons to draw your spider living in its home. Make sure to include all of its features.

Huntsman Spider

Quiz

Test Your Knowledge

1
Where do wheel spiders live?

2
Do huntsman spiders use webs to hunt?

3
How many eggs do huntsman spiders lay?

4
Which colors are most huntsman spiders?

5
Are huntsman spiders considered dangerous?

6
Which spiders are often called "banana spiders"?

7
Which sets of huntsman spider legs are the longest?

8
How many kinds of huntsman spiders are there?

ANSWERS 1. Deserts in Namibia 2. No 3. Up to 200 4. Brown or gray 5. No 6. Pantropical huntsman spiders 7. The front legs 8. About 1,200

Key Words

adaptations: changes in animals that make them better able to survive in their homes

fangs: sharp, pointed teeth or similar parts of an animal's mouth

habitat: the place where a plant or animal lives

molting: when an animal grows by shedding a layer of skin

pantropical: found across Earth's tropical regions

pedipalps: parts of an arachnid's mouth that are often used for grabbing or feeling

pests: animals that are considered annoying or frustrating by people

prey: animals that are hunted and eaten by other animals

sac: a pouch or bag that is either part of or made by an animal

sand dunes: a hill of sand on a beach or in a desert that is formed by wind

senses: the abilities used by an animal to understand and examine the world around it

spiderlings: baby spiders

tarantulas: a group of large, hairy spiders with downward-pointing fangs

vibrations: repeated shaking motions

Index

Get the best of both worlds.

AV2 bridges the gap between print and digital.

The expandable resources toolbar enables quick access to content including **videos**, **audio**, **activities**, **weblinks**, **slideshows**, **quizzes**, and **key words**.

Animated videos make static images come alive.

Resource icons on each page help readers to further **explore key concepts**.

Published by AV2
14 Penn Plaza, 9th Floor New York, NY 10122
Website: www.av2books.com

Library of Congress Control Number: 2019957408

ISBN 978-1-7911-2308-6 (hardcover)
ISBN 978-1-7911-2309-3 (softcover)
ISBN 978-1-7911-2310-9 (multi-user eBook)
ISBN 978-1-7911-2311-6 (single-user eBook)

Printed in Guangzhou, China
1 2 3 4 5 6 7 8 9 0 24 23 22 21 20

052020
101119

Designer: Terry Paulhus Project Coordinator: John Willis

The publisher acknowledges Alamy, Getty Images, iStock, Minden Pictures, Shutterstock, and Wikimedia as its primary image suppliers for this title.